JASMINE WINTERBOURNE

The AI Threat

Second edition

This book was professionally typeset on Reedsy.
Find out more at reedsy.com

Contents

Introduction

1.1 Background

Artificial Intelligence (AI) has progressed from a niche area of computer science to a transformative force shaping global industries, societal structures, and human interactions. Once confined to academic research and narrow, rule-based systems like chess engines or spam filters, AI is now deeply embedded in the technologies that people use daily—voice assistants like Siri and Alexa, recommendation algorithms on platforms like Netflix and YouTube, predictive text in messaging apps, medical diagnostics, autonomous vehicles, and even judicial risk assessment tools. These technologies are not only optimizing operational efficiency; they are altering how individuals experience reality, interact with information, and engage with one another.

Over the past two years, AI capabilities have accelerated at an unprecedented rate, particularly through the emergence of large language models (LLMs) such as GPT-4, Google's Gemini, and Anthropic's Claude. These systems can interpret and generate text, images, audio, and video, forming a class of "foundation models" that serve as the core infrastructure for thousands of downstream applications. Their ability to generalize across tasks and domains has radically expanded the potential of AI, shifting it from a reactive tool to a proactive collaborator capable of independent generation, summarization, translation, and creative expression.

The convergence of multimodal learning, generative algorithms, and accessible interfaces has led to AI tools being adopted not only by researchers and enterprises, but also by individuals, small businesses, and public institutions. In healthcare, AI assists with radiology interpretation, drug discovery, and remote diagnostics. In finance, it is used for algorithmic trading, credit scoring, and fraud detection. In education, AI tutors now personalize learning experiences for students across age groups and geographies. In entertainment, it creates music, art, and even interactive narratives that blur the line between creator and consumer.

These innovations are reshaping entire sectors—but they are also raising urgent societal questions. AI systems now play a role in shaping what people see, believe, and trust. They influence social media feeds, political discourse, customer experiences, and employment decisions. As a result, the discussion around AI has shifted from technical feasibility to societal consequence. Public and scholarly attention has moved beyond automation and job loss to include issues such as digital authenticity (can we trust what we see and hear?), human creativity (what makes human expression unique?), ethical agency (who is accountable for AI decisions?), and algorithmic governance (how should AI be regulated?).

Furthermore, as generative AI tools become capable of producing text, images, and voices indistinguishable from real content, there is a growing concern about their potential to manipulate public opinion, impersonate individuals, and erode trust in information ecosystems. The influence of AI on shaping personal identity, cultural narratives, institutional processes, and geopolitical dynamics underscores the need for a holistic and interdisciplinary approach to understanding and managing this technology.

1.2 Objectives

This dissertation revisits the pros and cons of AI in light of recent technological leaps and societal shifts. It aims to provide a comprehensive and up-to-date analysis of AI's societal, economic, and ethical impact, with a particular focus on developments from 2023 to 2025—a period that has witnessed rapid mainstream adoption of generative AI and the first wave of regulatory responses.

The study seeks to:

- Assess the transformative potential of AI across sectors such as healthcare, finance, education, public services, and the creative industries.
- Evaluate the emerging risks associated with algorithmic bias, surveillance, misinformation, privacy invasion, and the erosion of democratic institutions.
- Understand how AI compares to previous technological revolutions—such as the Industrial Revolution and the Information Age—in terms of social disruption, labour displacement, and adaptation mechanisms.
- Explore how new forms of human-AI collaboration are reshaping creative processes, decision-making frameworks, and knowledge production.
- Identify strategies for designing governance structures, legal frameworks, and educational initiatives that promote

equitable and responsible AI deployment.

1.3 Research Questions

- What are the updated benefits and drawbacks of AI in critical sectors such as healthcare, finance, education, and creative industries?
- How do recent advancements compare to past transformative technologies in terms of societal disruption and adaptation?
- What ethical risks have become more prominent in the past two years, particularly in the domains of bias, misinformation, and surveillance?
- How is AI influencing employment trends, skill requirements, and economic inequality across different populations and regions?
- What policy frameworks and governance models are emerging globally to ensure the safe, equitable, and responsible development of AI?

1.4 Methodology

This study employs a mixed-methods approach, combining qualitative and quantitative analysis to capture the complexity and multifaceted nature of AI's impacts. The qualitative component includes an extensive review of peer-reviewed academic literature, industry whitepapers, government reports, and ethics guidelines published between 2020 and 2025. The quantitative component draws on labour market datasets, economic trend indicators, productivity metrics, and surveys on public perception.

To ground the research in real-world outcomes, updated case studies from 2023 to 2025 are used to examine AI implementation in sectors such as healthcare diagnostics, education technology, media production, and government services. These are supplemented by interviews with experts in AI research, public policy, corporate strategy, and digital ethics, providing multi-perspective insights. Historical analogies are drawn from major technological transformation periods, including the Industrial Revolution, the rise of electricity, and the digital age, to extract enduring patterns and cautionary lessons.

1.5 Significance of the Study

Understanding how AI's trajectory has changed in just two years is critical for adapting educational systems, economic strategies, governance policies, and public institutions in real time. The pace of AI advancement has outstripped many of the frameworks designed to manage it, resulting in a regulatory, ethical, and conceptual lag. This dissertation fills a critical gap by synthesizing the latest developments, risks, and opportunities into a cohesive framework for action.

This study offers stakeholders—policymakers, educators, businesses, creatives, and the general public—a nuanced, evidence-based analysis of where AI is headed, the challenges it presents, and the pathways to responsible integration. It emphasizes the importance of proactive planning, interdisciplinary collaboration, public engagement, and inclusive policymaking. By focusing on the intersection of technology, ethics, and society, this research contributes to shaping an AI future that is not only innovative but also just, transparent, and human-centred.

Literature Review and Recent Developments

2.1 From Predictive Models to Generative Intelligence

The evolution from narrow, task-specific predictive models to highly generalised, generative AI systems marks one of the most profound shifts in the history of artificial intelligence. Predictive models—once limited to recommending products or flagging financial fraud—have now given way to versatile generative models capable of performing a wide array of cognitive tasks that previously required human input. This transformation has been driven by the development and deployment of large-scale foundation models such as Open AI's GPT-4, Google's Gemini, Anthropic's Claude, and powerful open-source alternatives like Meta's LLaMA and Mistral.

These models are "multimodal," meaning they can process and generate content across different forms—text, images, audio, video, and code—based on a single input prompt. Unlike earlier AI systems that were trained for narrow purposes, generative AI models are trained on vast corpora of internet text, visual data, and even code repositories, allowing them to produce highly coherent and contextually aware outputs. This has effectively transformed AI from a back-end analytical tool into a front-line collaborator across sectors.

In professional contexts, generative AI is revolutionising workflows. Legal professionals use AI to draft contracts, prepare case summaries, and conduct legal research. Journalists employ AI to summarize breaking news, fact-check content, and generate multilingual reports. In business and marketing, AI is driving automation in advertising, copywriting, audience targeting, and campaign analytics. Financial analysts now use generative models to draft reports, analyse trends, and simulate risk scenarios.

In the creative sector, the effects have been even more pronounced. AI-generated music, poetry, screenplays, digital artwork, and even fashion designs are being used in professional production pipelines. Tools such as Mid-journey, DALL·E, and Runway ML allow creators to produce high-quality visuals with a fraction of the time and resources once required. In the film and gaming industries, generative tools are now aiding in concept art, voice synthesis, storyboarding, and character generation, changing how media is conceived and produced.

In education, generative AI is being applied to create personalized learning experiences, adaptive testing, curriculum development, and tutoring. AI-powered platforms can generate explanations, answer questions, provide feedback, and adapt lesson plans in real time based on learner performance. This has opened up possibilities for more equitable and scalable education, particularly in underserved regions.

However, this transition from predictive to generative intelligence has sparked complex debates about authorship, authenticity, and originality. Since AI-generated content often mimics human style and output with remarkable precision, the distinction between human and machine authorship has become increasingly blurred. This has led to disputes over copyright, intellectual property rights, and the legal status of AI-generated works. Major lawsuits have been filed against AI developers for using copyrighted material in model training without explicit consent from content creators.

More fundamentally, the rise of generative AI has raised epistemological concerns: if machines can convincingly fabricate information or simulate expertise, how do we define and verify truth in an AI-mediated environment? The issue of "hallucinations"—confident but inaccurate outputs—remains unresolved. AI systems can generate plausible-sounding but factually incorrect statements, which, when uncritically accepted, can contribute to misinformation, misdiagnoses, and flawed decision-making.

To navigate these challenges, the field is moving toward human-AI collaboration frameworks. These encourage the use of generative AI as a tool for amplification rather than automation—enhancing human creativity and productivity while maintaining oversight, ethical standards, and accountability. Interpretability tools, explain ability dashboards, and responsible design principles are also becoming integral to the deployment of these systems.

Ultimately, the transition to generative AI has expanded the scope of what machines can do, pushing the boundaries of automation and creativity. But it has also introduced new layers of social, ethical, and cognitive complexity, making it imperative for policymakers, developers, and users to approach these technologies with a balanced mix of enthusiasm, caution, and critical inquiry.

2.2 Economic and Labour Market Impacts

Between 2023 and 2025, the economic influence of AI has become not just more visible but more deeply embedded in both public and private sectors. As generative and multimodal AI tools mature, they have shifted from experimental technologies to critical components of business infrastructure. Companies in logistics, manufacturing, legal services, and even creative industries now rely on AI to streamline processes, reduce operational costs, and increase productivity. AI is no longer viewed as a futuristic disruption—it is now a business imperative.

The nature of work has begun to shift accordingly. While fears of mass unemployment due to automation remain valid, the current impact has largely been sector-specific and role-specific. Repetitive, predictable, and routine jobs—particularly in content moderation, customer service, data entry, basic coding, and transcription—are among the most affected. AI-driven chatbots have replaced human agents in many first-line support roles, while automated systems now handle document review, invoice processing, and even some diagnostic functions in healthcare.

At the same time, a new wave of job creation is taking place. Roles such as prompt engineers, AI ethicists, model fine-tuners, data annotators, and human-in-the-loop supervisors have emerged. These jobs focus on guiding, training, and interpreting AI systems, ensuring their outputs are relevant, accurate, and ethically aligned. Furthermore, the need for educators and trainers who can teach AI literacy and upskill the workforce has surged.

Labour market polarization has also intensified. Workers in high-skill, digital-native professions benefit the most, while those in lower-skill roles without access to digital tools are more vulnerable to displacement. This has deepened existing socioeconomic divides, particularly in countries and regions with uneven access to digital infrastructure.

According to the World Economic Forum's 2024 Future of Jobs report, nearly 40% of global workers will need to reskill or upskill by 2030 to remain employable in an AI-driven economy. Many governments have responded by launching national AI education programs, apprenticeship models, and public-private reskilling initiatives. However, the effectiveness of these programs varies significantly depending on political will, funding, and coordination between industry and academia.

Crucially, the long-term economic impact of AI will depend not only on automation, but also on augmentation—how well AI can empower human workers to do more, faster, and with greater precision. Studies from McKinsey and PwC suggest that when deployed responsibly, AI can contribute trillions to global GDP by increasing productivity and enabling innovation. But these gains must be managed equitably to avoid entrenching inequalities and labour displacement.

2.3 Ethics, Trust, and Transparency

The rise of generative and decision-making AI has amplified ethical and societal concerns that were once confined to academic circles but are now at the forefront of public discourse. One of the most persistent issues is algorithmic bias. Despite advances in fairness-aware machine learning, bias continues to manifest in hiring algorithms, facial recognition systems, criminal justice risk assessments, and healthcare diagnostics—often leading to discriminatory outcomes for marginalized groups.

A key challenge is that AI systems learn patterns from historical data, which often contain implicit or explicit biases. When these patterns are replicated in automated decisions, they can reinforce existing inequities. Bias audits, fairness metrics, and third-party evaluations are becoming more common, but the technical and legal standards for fairness remain fragmented across jurisdictions.

Transparency is another urgent concern. Many state-of-the-art models—especially large language models—are considered "black boxes" because their decision-making processes are difficult to interpret even for their developers. Explain ability tools like SHAP, LIME, and integrated gradients are being used to analyse model behaviour, but they often fall short of providing user-friendly transparency for non-experts. This opacity undermines accountability and user trust.

Privacy concerns have surged as AI systems increasingly rely on large-scale datasets scraped from the internet or collected from user interactions. These datasets may include personal information without proper consent. High-profile lawsuits have been filed against AI companies for allegedly violating privacy laws, including those related to biometric data and copyrighted content. In response, techniques like differential privacy, federated learning, and synthetic data generation are gaining traction as privacy-preserving alternatives.

The spread of misinformation and synthetic content—such as deep fakes—has reached unprecedented levels. In 2024, multiple geopolitical crises were exacerbated by AI-generated fake news and falsified audio recordings. In response, governments and tech companies have initiated watermarking and digital provenance strategies to authenticate media. The C2PA (Coalition for Content Provenance and Authenticity) has emerged as a leading consortium in setting standards for content verification.

Ethical frameworks such as the OECD's AI Principles, UNESCO's AI Ethics Recommendation, and national strategies like Canada's Directive on Automated Decision-Making have begun to shape how AI is governed. However, implementation remains inconsistent, and enforcement mechanisms are still developing. Ethical AI development now requires not just technical expertise but also cross-disciplinary collaboration with ethicists, sociologists, legal scholars, and affected communities.

2.4 Policy and Governance Trends

As AI moves from labs to mainstream society, governments around the world are racing to establish coherent and enforceable governance frameworks. The European Union has taken a pioneering role with the EU AI Act (formally adopted in 2024), which classifies AI applications into four risk tiers—unacceptable, high, limited, and minimal—and applies escalating regulatory obligations accordingly.

High-risk systems, such as those used in law enforcement, employment, education, and critical infrastructure, must undergo rigorous conformity assessments, maintain technical documentation, and implement human oversight mechanisms. The Act also bans certain AI uses outright, such as social scoring by governments and real-time biometric surveillance in public spaces. It is widely regarded as the most comprehensive AI regulation to date and is influencing regulatory efforts globally.

In the United States, AI governance is more fragmented but evolving. The 2023 Executive Order on the Safe, Secure, and Trustworthy Development and Use of Artificial Intelligence introduced mandatory reporting on AI safety, guidelines for federal procurement, and research investments in AI safety and fairness. Individual states, such as California and New York, are also drafting their own AI-specific laws.

Multilateral initiatives have emerged to address the global nature of AI. The G7's Hiroshima Process, OECD's AI policy observatory, and the United Nations' advisory group on global AI governance are all working to harmonize standards, promote transparency, and reduce regulatory arbitrage. However, geopolitical tensions—particularly between the U.S., China, and the EU—complicate efforts to establish universal norms.

Emerging economies face unique challenges and opportunities. Countries such as India, Brazil, and Kenya are investing in sovereign AI ecosystems to avoid dependency on foreign platforms and ensure that local values and data sovereignty are respected. At the same time, they must balance innovation with the need for safeguards, especially in sectors like healthcare, agriculture, and education.

A recurring governance theme is the concentration of power among a few tech giants who develop and control the infrastructure behind foundation models. This has led to discussions about "AI monopolies" and calls for open access, transparency in training data, and democratization of AI capabilities. The governance of these foundation models—how they are built, who funds them, and who is accountable for their outputs—has become a focal point for global policy debates.

As governance efforts mature, the challenge will be to maintain flexibility and adaptability in regulatory frameworks without stifling innovation. Future governance models are likely to be dynamic, iterative, and collaborative—designed not as rigid rulebooks, but as evolving compacts between technology developers, governments, and the public.

Comparisons to Past Technological Shifts

3.1 The Industrial Revolution

The Industrial Revolution, spanning the late 18th and early 19th centuries, is often cited as the first major technological disruption to economic and social life. It marked the transition from agrarian economies to industrialised, urban societies through innovations such as the steam engine, mechanised textile production, and mass manufacturing. This shift redefined the nature of work, replacing artisanal and manual labour with machine-driven processes and assembly lines. Similarly, the advent of artificial intelligence—particularly since 2020—can be understood as a new wave of disruption, this time targeting cognitive and knowledge-based labour.

Just as the steam engine displaced the manual labourer, AI is now automating tasks once thought to be the exclusive domain of the human intellect: writing, designing, diagnosing, teaching, and decision-making. This shift is redefining what constitutes a "skilled" worker. Clerical workers, entry-level creatives, paralegals, and even some junior software developers now find their tasks partially or wholly outsourced to algorithms. The

Industrial Revolution eventually gave rise to new job sectors, but only after a turbulent period marked by social unrest, unemployment, and widening inequality—issues echoed in today's AI transition.

Moreover, the ripple effects of industrialisation transformed not only the workplace, but also the structure of entire societies. Urbanisation intensified, education systems evolved to prepare workers for industrial roles, and infrastructure adapted to support new modes of production and transport. In parallel, AI is now reconfiguring digital infrastructure, reshaping educational curricula to include coding and AI literacy, and prompting governments to rethink how cities, labour markets, and communication systems are organised.

A key lesson from the Industrial Revolution is the importance of proactive social policy. As the 19th century progressed, governments and societies responded to industrial upheaval by introducing child labour laws, public education, labour unions, and early forms of social security. These reforms helped ease the societal transition and set the stage for inclusive growth. In the present AI context, the equivalent would be large-scale investment in reskilling and upskilling programs, robust unemployment protections for displaced workers, and ethical labour standards for AI-assisted jobs. Without such measures, the automation of cognitive tasks risks deepening inequality and fuelling social division.

The Industrial Revolution also prompted debates about the human role in a mechanised world—debates that resonate today. Philosophers, economists, and social critics of the time asked whether machines were merely tools or whether they would fundamentally redefine human agency. AI poses similar existential questions: What does it mean to be creative, to make decisions, or to hold expertise when machines can simulate these functions? Just as industrialisation catalysed a reevaluation of labour and human worth, AI is compelling us to rethink intelligence, authorship, and even personhood. The challenge, then as now, lies not in resisting technological change, but in shaping its trajectory to uphold human dignity and shared prosperity.

3.2 The Computer and Internet Age

The second major point of comparison is the computer revolution of the mid-to-late 20th century, followed by the rise of the Internet in the 1990s and early 2000s. These technologies introduced automation into office environments, digitised communication, and created global networks of information sharing and commerce. Much like AI today, these earlier innovations were initially met with both awe and scepticism. They promised improved productivity, access to knowledge, and new modes of connection—but also introduced new forms of inequality, surveillance, and information overload.

One critical difference lies in the pace and scale of disruption. The personal computer took decades to become ubiquitous; the Internet followed a similarly gradual diffusion pattern. In contrast, generative AI systems have gone from lab prototypes to mass adoption within a few short years. For instance, Open AI's ChatGPT reached 100 million users in just two months—making it the fastest-growing consumer application in history. This exponential pace means that individuals, businesses, and governments have less time to adapt, increasing the risk of harm and exacerbating institutional lag.

Moreover, AI systems are not merely platforms for communication or calculation—they are autonomous agents capable of generating content, making predictions, and influencing human decisions. This introduces a deeper level of epistemic risk than previous technologies. AI can produce false but plausible information—so-called "hallucinations"—that users may take at face value. This differs from the misinformation challenges of the early Internet, where humans were still the primary creators of content. With AI, machines are not just amplifiers of information but generators of it, challenging traditional methods of fact-checking, source validation, and editorial oversight.

Another point of divergence is the centralisation of power. While the early Internet was shaped by open protocols and a spirit of decentralisation, the AI landscape is currently dominated by a small number of powerful tech firms that control access to foundation models, compute infrastructure, and massive training datasets. This creates new forms of economic and informational dependency, raising antitrust and governance concerns. Furthermore, these gatekeepers are shaping the direction of AI research, cultural narratives, and even political influence, creating a digital oligopoly that raises urgent questions about transparency, accountability, and democratic control.

Nonetheless, there are also positive lessons to be drawn from the computer age. The rise of digital literacy programs, open-source software, and online learning platforms showed that widespread access and education could democratise new technologies. Similarly, public AI literacy, transparency initiatives, and ethical design practices could ensure that AI benefits are broadly distributed. There is growing momentum behind calls for open models, community-driven AI development, and "commons-based" technological infrastructure that would mirror the early open ethos of the web.

Additionally, the integration of the Internet into education, business, and healthcare showed that humans are capable of adapting to transformative technologies over time—provided that infrastructure, regulation, and cultural norms evolve in parallel. Just as society adapted to the computer and Internet revolutions through innovation, policy, and cultural change, a similar adaptation is possible with AI—provided it is approached thoughtfully, inclusively, and with a commitment to human flourishing.

Emerging Ethical and Social Considerations

4.1 Algorithmic Bias and Equity

Algorithmic bias remains one of the most persistent and challenging issues in AI development. As AI systems are deployed in increasingly sensitive domains—such as healthcare diagnostics, credit lending, predictive policing, and job recruitment—the consequences of bias can be severe and far-reaching. Numerous studies and real-world examples have demonstrated that AI models trained on skewed or incomplete data can reinforce and even exacerbate structural inequalities based on race, gender, socioeconomic status, and geography.

For instance, healthcare algorithms used in the United States to allocate patient care resources have been found to systematically underestimate the needs of Black patients. In hiring, automated resume screening tools have penalized candidates based on gendered language or gaps in employment history, disproportionately affecting women and caregivers. In finance, credit scoring models have exhibited discriminatory patterns when trained on datasets reflecting historical redlining or unequal access to loans. Predictive policing tools have directed increased surveillance toward low-income and minority neighbourhoods, further entrenching cycles of marginalization and criminalization.

To address these issues, inclusion and diversity in training datasets have become a key focus. However, simply increasing dataset size is insufficient—what matters is the representativeness and contextual accuracy of the data. Organizations are increasingly investing in bias audits, algorithmic impact assessments, and third-party evaluations. Tools such as Fairness Indicators, Aequitas, IBM's AI Fairness 360 Toolkit, and Google's What-If Tool are being deployed to identify and mitigate disparate impacts across demographic groups. Ethical AI frameworks now often include metrics for equal opportunity, disparate impact ratio, calibration across groups, and counterfactual fairness.

Regulatory bodies are beginning to respond. The EU AI Act, for example, mandates strict scrutiny of high-risk AI applications, including those used in education, employment, and law enforcement. It requires providers of these systems to conduct conformity assessments, provide documentation of risk mitigation procedures, and maintain records for auditability. Some U.S. states—such as California, New York, and Illinois—are introducing legislation requiring companies to disclose and evaluate the fairness of their algorithms, especially when used for consequential decisions in hiring and housing. However, global standards for algorithmic fairness remain fragmented, and enforcement mechanisms are still in development or vary in scope and rigour.

Beyond compliance and audits, some organizations are turning to participatory design models, where affected communities are actively involved in the development and evaluation of AI systems. This approach promotes transparency, ensures that context-specific needs are taken into account, and builds trust between developers and end users. There is also a growing movement to create "ethics by design" methodologies that embed fairness, accountability, and transparency directly into AI development pipelines from the outset rather than treating them as afterthoughts.

Leading academic institutions and research labs are now incorporating ethical AI design into their engineering, law, and data science curricula. Interdisciplinary education is becoming more common, with programs combining computer science, philosophy, sociology, public policy, and law. These initiatives reflect a broader understanding that technical excellence must be matched by social responsibility and cultural awareness.

Technology companies are also beginning to form internal ethics boards, release responsible AI guidelines, and commit to open publishing of fairness-related research. Some firms are even creating roles like "AI fairness lead" or "chief ethics officer" to integrate equity considerations across all stages of the AI lifecycle—from problem formulation and dataset curation to deployment and feedback loops.

Ultimately, ensuring equity in AI requires interdisciplinary collaboration among technologists, ethicists, sociologists, legal scholars, educators, activists, and affected communities. It also necessitates cultural change within organizations, emphasizing ethical responsibility alongside technical performance, long-term accountability over short-term gains, and transparency over proprietary secrecy. Without sustained attention to these issues, AI risks becoming a force that entrenches, rather than alleviates, social inequalities.

4.2 Data Privacy and Surveillance

The vast amounts of data required to train modern AI systems raise serious concerns about privacy and surveillance. These systems are often trained on web-scraped data, user-generated content, personal communications, biometric data, and more—frequently without the informed consent of the individuals whose information is used. This raises legal, ethical, and reputational risks, especially as public awareness and regulatory scrutiny increase.

Regulations such as the General Data Protection Regulation (GDPR) in the European Union and the California Consumer Privacy Act (CC PA) in the United States have introduced principles of data minimization, user consent, and the right to be forgotten. The EU AI Act builds on these frameworks by requiring transparency and traceability in data collection and model training processes. However, enforcement remains uneven across jurisdictions, and compliance is often difficult to verify, especially for open-source or globally distributed systems.

Emerging technical solutions aim to address privacy concerns while maintaining model performance. Federated learning, for instance, allows AI models to be trained across multiple decentralized devices or servers holding local data samples—without exchanging the data itself. This reduces the risk of centralized data breaches and enhances user control. Differential privacy techniques add statistical noise to data during training to obscure individual identities, while synthetic data generation creates artificial datasets that mimic the structure of real data without exposing personal information.

Nevertheless, challenges remain. Federated and privacy-preserving AI approaches often involve trade-offs in terms of computational efficiency and model accuracy. Moreover, in authoritarian regimes or surveillance-heavy contexts, AI technologies are increasingly being used to monitor citizens, predict dissent, and suppress opposition. This has led to growing concerns over the use of facial recognition, social scoring systems, and mass biometric surveillance.

Ensuring that privacy is not an afterthought but a core design principle of AI requires coordinated legal frameworks, technical innovation, and public pressure to hold institutions accountable.

4.3 The Deep fake Dilemma

Deep fake technology—powered by generative adversarial networks (GANs) and diffusion models—has advanced rapidly in both quality and accessibility. AI-generated audio, video, and image content can now closely mimic real individuals' voices, faces, and mannerisms, often with minimal data inputs. This has sparked a global ethical crisis, as deep fakes blur the boundaries between reality and fiction.

In 2024 alone, multiple political events and election cycles were disrupted by the spread of deep fake videos. These included falsified speeches by world leaders, fabricated scandalous footage of candidates, and audio clips of supposed private conversations. In addition to political manipulation, deep fakes are being used in revenge porn, identity theft, financial fraud, and misinformation campaigns. Their accessibility on mobile apps and consumer platforms makes them a threat at scale.

The response from lawmakers and technologists has been swift but varied. Legislative actions in the U.S., UK, EU, India, and Southeast Asia are aiming to criminalize malicious deep fake creation and mandate content labelling. Meanwhile, tech companies are working on watermarking technologies, blockchain-based verification systems, and content provenance protocols (such as the Coalition for Content Provenance and Authenticity, or C2PA) to track and authenticate digital media.

Academic researchers and AI developers are also creating detection algorithms capable of identifying signs of synthetic manipulation, though these systems are locked in an arms race with increasingly sophisticated generators. The risk of "zero trust" environments—where all content is suspect—has major implications for journalism, law, and public discourse.

Addressing the deep fake dilemma requires a multi-layered strategy: legal penalties for misuse, investment in detection and verification technologies, media literacy campaigns for the public, and ethical guidelines for content creators and developers. Without such measures, the erosion of informational trust may undermine democratic institutions and social cohesion.

4.4 Emotional and Moral Reasoning

Despite their linguistic fluency and growing multimodal capabilities, AI systems fundamentally lack emotional intelligence, self-awareness, and the capacity for moral reasoning. They can simulate empathy and ethical discourse, but these outputs are generated statistically—based on patterns in training data—not on any intrinsic understanding of emotion or values.

This limitation has serious implications in high-stakes domains where human judgment, emotional nuance, and moral sensitivity are essential. For instance, in healthcare, AI systems may assist with diagnosis but cannot provide the empathetic communication required to deliver bad news or guide patients through complex care decisions. In education, while AI tutors can offer personalized content, they lack the relational understanding necessary to mentor, motivate, or respond to emotional cues. In governance or law, AI can analyse case law and recommend policy options, but it cannot weigh ethical trade-offs or incorporate compassion into justice.

To address these gaps, researchers are exploring hybrid approaches that combine rule-based systems with machine learning. These systems embed explicit ethical frameworks—such as utilitarianism or deontology—into algorithmic logic, allowing for more structured ethical decision-making. However, these models still lack the lived experience, cultural context, and reflective capacity of human morality.

There is growing recognition that AI should support, rather than replace, moral judgment. Human-in-the-loop systems, ethical oversight committees, and value-sensitive design are being promoted to ensure that AI tools are aligned with societal values and human needs. Emotional AI—systems that attempt to detect and respond to human emotions—is also advancing, particularly in customer service, marketing, and wearable tech. However, these systems raise additional concerns about emotional manipulation, consent, and authenticity.

Ultimately, the emotional and moral limitations of AI underscore the importance of preserving human agency in critical decision-making processes. While machines can augment cognition and automate routine reasoning, they cannot—and should not—replace the human capacity for empathy, ethical deliberation, and moral accountability.

Economic Trends and Workforce Adaptation

5.1 Reskilling at Scale

The rapid integration of AI into industries has dramatically accelerated the demand for large-scale reskilling programs. With tasks across finance, healthcare, logistics, legal services, creative sectors, customer service, and education increasingly automated or augmented by AI technologies, workers in both blue-collar and white-collar roles are being pushed to adapt or risk obsolescence. The pace of technological change is compressing learning timelines and reshaping traditional career paths, forcing a paradigm shift in how societies and institutions approach workforce development.

Governments, educational institutions, non-profit organizations, and private enterprises are now responding with a multi-pronged approach to retraining and upskilling. Countries such as India, Singapore, Germany, Finland, and several EU member states have launched ambitious, government-funded programs aimed at building AI fluency across the population. India's "Future Skills Prime" platform, developed in partnership with NASSCOM, provides structured AI and digital literacy courses to millions of professionals and students in both metropolitan and rural areas. Singapore's "Skills Future" initiative not only supports AI training for workers but also encourages lifelong learning through vouchers and online platforms, fostering a national culture of continuous education.

The European Union's "Digital Education Action Plan" and the "Pact for Skills" offer long-term strategies for cross-border cooperation in workforce transformation. These initiatives are aimed at improving access to digital and AI education through partnerships between governments, industry, and academia. They focus on inclusivity, ensuring that traditionally underserved communities—including women, minorities, and rural populations—are not left behind in the AI transition.

In the corporate sphere, major employers such as Amazon, Microsoft, Google, IBM, Accenture, and PwC have committed substantial resources to internal reskilling initiatives. Amazon's "Career Choice" program provides funding and access to certified training for front-line workers in fields like cloud computing, AI fundamentals, and IT support. Microsoft's global skilling initiative, launched in collaboration with LinkedIn Learning and GitHub, aims to train over 25 million people in digital skills, with a special emphasis on low-income and displaced workers. These programs are increasingly emphasizing hybrid competencies—teaching workers how to leverage AI tools to enhance their own productivity rather than view the technology as a threat.

Despite growing momentum, reskilling at scale presents numerous challenges. Many workers face barriers such as limited access to broadband, lack of digital literacy, financial constraints, or time scarcity due to care-giving or multiple jobs. These barriers disproportionately affect rural residents, older adults, immigrants, and those in the informal economy. To close these gaps, NGOs, public-private partnerships, and philanthropic foundations are stepping in with targeted interventions—developing mobile learning units, local training hubs, and flexible micro-credentialing systems that cater to these populations.

The ultimate success of reskilling programs hinges not only on content delivery but also on systemic support. This includes career guidance, mentorship, recognized certification pathways, internship opportunities, and strong linkages to real employment outcomes. Without these supports, there is a risk that reskilling initiatives will be underutilized or ineffective, exacerbating existing inequalities. Governments and companies must treat reskilling not as a one-time response, but as an ongoing societal investment.

5.2 Polarization of Opportunity

While AI holds the potential to drive widespread economic growth and enhance human capabilities, the current distribution of benefits remains heavily skewed. One of the most pressing concerns among economists, development experts, and labour advocates is that AI will deepen socioeconomic divides both within and across national borders. High-skilled, digitally fluent workers—especially those in urban tech hubs of North America, Europe, and East Asia—are currently the main beneficiaries of AI integration. They gain access to new tools, higher productivity, elevated roles, and rising wages in AI-adjacent fields.

By contrast, workers with lower digital literacy, limited access to formal education, and few reskilling opportunities are at risk of being left behind. Roles that require routine cognitive or physical tasks—such as data entry, basic accounting, call centre operations, retail clerks, and logistics coordinators—are increasingly vulnerable to automation. Many of these jobs have historically served as entry points into the workforce, particularly in developing countries and among marginalized populations. As generative AI displaces freelance content creators, translators, and customer service agents, the economic safety nets in many regions are being tested.

The digital divide underpins much of this polarization. Across the Global South, large segments of the population lack access to affordable high-speed internet, up-to-date hardware, or digital education. Moreover, existing AI systems often reflect and amplify Western-centric perspectives, further marginalizing voices from linguistically and culturally diverse backgrounds. Low-resource languages, indigenous communities, and localized social contexts are frequently omitted from training datasets, creating systems that are blind to their needs and realities.

To reduce this polarization, proactive policy interventions are essential. Governments must invest in broadband infrastructure, expand access to devices, integrate AI literacy into school curricula, and ensure equitable funding for public education. Scholarship programs, women-in-tech initiatives, and partnerships with local educators can further bridge the digital skills gap. Global institutions such as the World Bank, IMF, UNESCO, and the UNDP are starting to prioritize AI inclusion in their development agendas, advocating for frameworks that promote responsible and inclusive deployment.

Private companies also play a pivotal role. There is a growing call for tech firms to expand access to their platforms, offer tiered services for low-income users, open-source foundational tools, and engage in inclusive design processes. Companies like Meta and Hugging Face are exploring "low-resource" LLMs that require less computational power and training data, making them more accessible for deployment in less-developed regions. Additionally, tech incubators and accelerators in emerging markets—such as Nairobi's iHub or Nigeria's Co-Creation Hub—are empowering local entrepreneurs to develop AI tools tailored to their communities.

Failure to address the growing polarization of opportunity could result in the emergence of a two-tier AI economy: one where affluent societies benefit from AI-driven innovation and efficiency, while lower-income regions fall further behind. Closing this gap requires global coordination, inclusive policymaking, and public-private partnerships committed to democratizing AI's benefits.

5.3 Entrepreneurial Growth

AI is also catalysing a new wave of entrepreneurial energy, with startups and small-scale innovators at the forefront of developing domain-specific applications, platform solutions, and human-centred technologies. This wave of innovation spans sectors including healthcare, education, agriculture, financial services, climate technology, creative industries, and manufacturing. The availability of open-source models, cloud-based APIs, and public research datasets has significantly lowered the entry barriers for aspiring entrepreneurs.

In the healthcare domain, startups are leveraging AI to power diagnostic imaging tools, predictive analytics for chronic diseases, AI-driven telehealth platforms, and mental health chatbots. In education, companies are building adaptive learning software, content recommendation engines, and AI-powered grading tools. Startups like ScribeSense, Duolingo, and Sana Labs are developing tools that personalize learning experiences and scale tutoring resources for underserved populations.

Agritech ventures are using AI for drone-assisted crop monitoring, real-time weather forecasting, and livestock health tracking. Fintech startups are deploying machine learning for credit scoring, fraud detection, and personalized financial planning, especially targeting unbanked populations in emerging economies. AI is also making inroads into environmental conservation, with startups using satellite data and computer vision to monitor deforestation, track illegal fishing, and model climate risks.

Venture capital remains bullish on AI, with global investments in AI startups surpassing $100 billion in 2024. Major firms like Sequoia Capital, Andreessen Horowitz, Lightspeed Ventures, and SoftBank Vision Fund continue to support high-growth startups building LLM-based services, vertical AI solutions, and synthetic data platforms. At the same time, growing concerns about a speculative "AI bubble" are prompting more scrutiny on monetization strategies, technical defensibility, and long-term impact.

Governments are also stepping up to support entrepreneurial growth through targeted incentives. The UK's "AI Sector Deal" includes investments in research labs, accelerators, and AI PhDs. France's "AI for Humanity" strategy funds early-stage ventures and ethical AI development. The U.S. CHIPS and Science Act includes billions in funding for AI research and commercialization pathways. Canada's Pan-Canadian AI Strategy, centred around hubs like MILA and the Vector Institute, has created fertile ground for startup growth.

Grassroots entrepreneurship is thriving in developing regions, with innovators in Kenya, Nigeria, Brazil, and Indonesia building hyper-local AI solutions. From AI-driven translation platforms for indigenous languages to low-cost diagnostic kits powered by edge computing, these projects demonstrate that local knowledge and community input are essential ingredients in successful AI innovation. Non-profit incubators, university accelerators, and diaspora funding networks are further expanding the pipeline for inclusive entrepreneurship.

Overall, AI entrepreneurship represents both an economic engine and a democratizing force—one capable of generating wealth, creating jobs, and solving local and global challenges. However, to reach its full potential, the entrepreneurial ecosystem must be supported by robust infrastructure, inclusive policies, mentorship opportunities, open innovation platforms, and thoughtful regulation that encourages experimentation while protecting public interest.

Public Perception and Societal Impacts

As AI systems grow in complexity and visibility, their impact on societal attitudes, trust in institutions, and the cultural fabric of everyday life is intensifying. Public perception is no longer shaped merely by media portrayals of futuristic robots—it is grounded in direct, frequent interactions with real AI tools, from voice assistants and automated chatbots to recommendation algorithms and facial recognition systems. This evolving relationship has generated new psychological, social, and political dynamics that influence how communities engage with AI technologies and the organizations that produce them.

Public acceptance of AI hinges on a multidimensional interplay of knowledge, experience, and trust. In many cases, people are unaware they are even using AI—recommendation feeds on Netflix, autocorrect on phones, and fraud detection in banking all rely on machine learning algorithms, yet they operate invisibly. This creates a paradox where AI becomes ubiquitous yet misunderstood, leading to both overestimation and underestimation of its capabilities and threats.

In democratic societies, the perception of AI also intersects with broader anxieties about surveillance, data security, economic inequality, and the influence of corporate power. The concentration of AI capabilities in the hands of a few tech giants has provoked fears of monopolistic control over public knowledge, digital labour, and even political discourse. As AI begins to shape how news is delivered, how creative content is produced, and how decisions are made in healthcare, finance, and education, concerns about accountability and transparency are increasingly shaping public discourse.

At the same time, AI is being mythologized and anthropomorphized in popular media, creating a symbolic tension between fear and fascination. While dystopian narratives dominate some corners of science fiction, new generations of users are also exploring AI as a source of empowerment, collaboration, and even companionship. The societal impacts of AI are thus not only technological—they are emotional, cultural, and profoundly human.

Surveys conducted between 2023 and 2025 show that trust in AI is highly variable across regions and demographics. In countries with robust data protection laws and transparency standards, citizens are more likely to view AI positively. In contrast, in areas where algorithmic bias, misinformation, and digital exclusion have made headlines, scepticism and resistance are more pronounced. Religious, generational, and educational factors also influence how AI is perceived—with younger generations generally more comfortable experimenting with AI tools, and older populations expressing concern about displacement and surveillance.

Civic participation is emerging as a critical component of shaping AI's future. Community-led initiatives, public deliberation forums, AI citizen assemblies, and participatory design labs are being explored as methods for democratizing AI governance and fostering meaningful dialogue between developers, users, and regulators. As a result, the question is shifting from "What can AI do?" to "What kind of AI do we want?" This evolving public consciousness is essential for guiding responsible AI development and ensuring it reflects shared human values rather than purely technological ambition.

Ultimately, the societal impact of AI will depend as much on perception and culture as it will on code and infrastructure. Understanding and responding to public attitudes is not only a matter of communication—it is a foundational requirement for building inclusive, ethical, and sustainable AI systems in the years ahead.

6.1 Trust and Transparency

Trust in artificial intelligence remains one of the most crucial—and fragile—elements in the successful integration of AI into daily life. While AI systems are becoming increasingly pervasive, from voice assistants and recommendation engines to autonomous vehicles and generative chatbots, users often do not understand how these systems make decisions. This opacity has led to growing public scepticism and anxiety about AI's intentions, reliability, and accountability.

A major contributor to the trust deficit is the "black box" nature of many advanced AI systems, particularly deep learning models. These systems process vast amounts of data through complex mathematical layers, producing results that are difficult—even for experts—to interpret. As a result, there is a strong push across the industry for explain ability, or the ability to understand and articulate why a model produced a particular output.

Tools like SHAP (SHapley Additive exPlanations), LIME (Local Interpretable Model-Agnostic Explanations), and model-specific interpretability modules are now being integrated into AI development pipelines to make decisions more transparent to developers, regulators, and users. Transparency dashboards, such as those used by Google and Meta, allow users to view how their data is collected and how content is recommended or prioritized.

In the enterprise space, explain ability is not just an ethical issue—it's becoming a legal requirement. Financial institutions must now justify algorithmic decisions in credit scoring, fraud detection, and loan approvals. Healthcare providers using AI diagnostic tools must ensure transparency to patients and medical professionals. The EU AI Act requires that high-risk AI systems provide clear documentation on their functioning, data sources, and decision-making rationale.

Furthermore, trust in AI also depends on the consistency and fairness of outcomes. If a system demonstrates unpredictable behaviour or exhibits bias—such as disproportionately flagging certain demographic groups for fraud or denying services—it can quickly erode user confidence. Building trust, therefore, requires both technical transparency and robust performance.

Public engagement initiatives, including AI ethics forums, community workshops, and open-source transparency projects, are beginning to emerge as a way to foster dialogue and demystify AI. These efforts, while promising, are still in their infancy and need scaling to meet the demand for inclusive, informed public discourse.

6.2 Cultural and Creative Shifts

The rise of generative AI has triggered profound cultural and philosophical debates about the nature of creativity, authorship, and artistic value. Artists, musicians, writers, and film-makers are grappling with a rapidly changing creative landscape, where machines can now compose symphonies, write poetry, generate paintings, and craft photorealistic animations—all at the click of a button.

Some artists embrace AI as a collaborative tool that can enhance creativity and enable new forms of expression. They see AI not as a replacement, but as a creative partner—a source of inspiration, ideation, and experimentation. For example, visual artists are using tools like Mid journey and DALL·E to generate concept art, while writers experiment with AI co-writing tools to develop plot lines, dialogue, or even entire manuscripts. In music, platforms like AIVA and Amper Music allow creators to compose original scores in minutes, reshaping how soundtracks and jingles are produced.

Others, however, express deep concern about the devaluation of human creativity. As AI-generated content floods digital spaces, distinguishing between human-made and machine-made art becomes increasingly difficult. This has led to legal and ethical conflicts around ownership and intellectual property. Multiple lawsuits have emerged challenging whether AI-generated works can be copyrighted, and who holds the rights—the programmer, the user, or the model itself. The U.S. Copyright Office and international bodies are actively debating these issues, with no global consensus yet in place.

Moreover, the proliferation of AI content threatens to saturate markets, potentially reducing the demand for human artists, illustrators, and writers—particularly in commercial fields like advertising, publishing, and gaming. This could further concentrate power in the hands of companies that own and control generative AI models, making it harder for individual artists to compete.

At a deeper level, societies are rethinking what it means to create, to be original, and to express uniquely human experiences. Some argue that true creativity requires lived experience, emotional depth, and cultural context—elements AI lacks. Others see creativity as a process that can include any tool, human or machine. These debates are reshaping art education, ethics, and even museum and gallery practices.

AI is also influencing pop culture. Films, video games, and literature increasingly explore AI as characters, themes, and even co-creators. From sci-fi thrillers to interactive AI-based storytelling platforms, the boundaries between fiction, media, and technology are blurring in real time.

6.3 Digital Literacy

Despite the proliferation of AI tools and platforms, public understanding of how AI works remains remarkably low. This gap in knowledge poses a serious challenge to responsible adoption, as users often interact with AI systems without understanding their limitations, underlying logic, or potential for harm.

Many individuals assume that AI systems are objective, rational, and inherently trustworthy, when in fact they are shaped by biased training data, human-defined objectives, and technical limitations. Without proper digital literacy, users may misinterpret AI outputs as factual or authoritative, leading to poor decision-making in areas like health, finance, and education. Conversely, distrust may cause users to reject AI tools even when they could be beneficial.

To address this issue, a growing number of schools, universities, and civil society organizations are introducing AI literacy programs. These include curricula focused on the basics of machine learning, ethical implications, data stewardship, and critical thinking about technology. For example, Finland has implemented a national AI education program that encourages all citizens to take a free, accessible online course on AI fundamentals. Similar efforts are underway in Canada, the Netherlands, and South Korea.

Media literacy is also being expanded to include AI-related topics. Journalists and news outlets are increasingly responsible for explaining AI developments to the public in accessible, accurate terms. Non-profits and think tanks are producing open-source educational resources, explainer videos, and workshops aimed at empowering citizens to navigate the AI age with confidence.

There is a growing recognition that digital literacy must extend beyond technical skills to include ethical and civic dimensions. Understanding who builds AI, how it is trained, whose interests it serves, and how it can be challenged are essential components of a digitally literate society. Empowering users with this knowledge not only fosters responsible engagement but also strengthens democratic oversight of AI technologies.

In summary, public perception of AI is shaped by trust, cultural shifts, and the ability to understand and critique the systems that now influence every aspect of modern life. Addressing these societal impacts is just as critical as advancing the technology itself, and must remain central to any responsible

AI strategy.

Recommendations for the Future

7.1 Algorithmic Bias and Fairness

This section provides an in-depth analysis of algorithmic bias, emphasising the importance of fairness and equity in AI systems. It explores the root causes of prejudice and examines the potential consequences of biased AI algorithms. One of the leading causes of bias is the personal training data used to train AI models. If the training data is not diverse and representative of the population, the AI system may learn and perpetuate existing biases present in the data. Additionally, discrimination can arise from the design choices in developing the algorithms themselves.

Various strategies can be employed to mitigate bias and promote fairness in AI systems. One approach is ensuring the training data is diverse and inclusive, representing different demographics and perspectives. By incorporating a more comprehensive range of data, AI models can avoid perpetuating unfair biases. Moreover, algorithmic transparency is crucial for identifying and addressing discrimination. By making the decision-making process of AI algorithms transparent and understandable, it becomes possible to detect and rectify biases in the system. External audits and third-party evaluations can also help identify and mitigate bias in AI systems.

7.2 Privacy and Data Protection

Privacy concerns become significant as AI heavily relies on large amounts of data. This section explores the ethical considerations associated with data collection, storage, and usage in AI systems. It acknowledges the benefits of data-driven AI, such as personalised recommendations and improved decision-making, while highlighting the need to protect individual privacy rights.

Balancing the benefits of data-driven AI with privacy protection is a complex challenge. It involves ensuring that data is collected with informed consent and that individuals can control how their data is used. Regulatory frameworks, such as data protection laws and privacy regulations, play a crucial role in safeguarding personal information in the AI era. Additionally, privacy-enhancing technologies, such as differential privacy and secure multiparty computation, can enable sensitive data analysis while preserving privacy.

7.3 Accountability and Transparency

Transparency and accountability are essential for fostering trust in AI systems and addressing ethical concerns. This section explores the challenges of understanding and explaining the decision-making processes of AI algorithms, particularly in complex deep-learning models. Lack of transparency can hinder the identification and mitigation of bias and the detection of errors or unintended consequences.

To promote accountability and transparency in AI, it is essential to make AI development processes more open and accessible. This includes providing documentation and clear explanations of AI models and their decision-making processes. Interpretability techniques, such as explainable AI and model-agnostic methods, can help provide insights into the reasoning behind AI decisions. Moreover, involving multidisciplinary teams, including domain experts and ethicists, in developing and deploying AI systems can enhance transparency and ensure that ethical considerations are adequately addressed.

7.4 Human-Centric AI and the Future of Work

This section expands on human-centric AI, emphasising the importance of AI systems that augment human capabilities rather than replace humans. It explores the potential for AI to enhance human creativity, decision-making, and problem-solving. By delegating repetitive and mundane tasks to AI systems, humans can focus on tasks requiring unique human skills, such as empathy, complex problem-solving, and creativity.

Reimagining work in the AI era involves identifying the tasks and roles that can be enhanced by AI technologies and leveraging AI as a tool to support human workers. This requires retraining and upskilling the workforce to adapt to the changing nature of work. Individuals can remain relevant in the job market by focusing on lifelong learning and acquiring skills that complement AI technologies. Moreover, creating inclusive and supportive work environments that foster collaboration between humans and AI systems is essential for successful integration and adoption.

In conclusion, addressing algorithmic bias, privacy concerns, ensuring accountability, and adopting a human-centric approach are critical in realising the full potential of AI while safeguarding ethical principles and societal values. By incorporating these considerations into the development and deployment of AI systems, society can strive towards a future where AI technologies serve as tools for positive change and human empowerment.

Economic Impacts and Employment Implications

8.1 Job Displacement and Reskilling Challenges

In this section, a detailed analysis is provided regarding the potential impacts of AI on employment, with a focus on job displacement and the challenges associated with reskilling and upskilling the workforce.

The discussion begins by examining various studies and research that shed light on the sectors most vulnerable to automation. Certain occupations and tasks that are routine and repetitive are at a higher risk of being automated, which can lead to the displacement of workers in those roles. However, it is essential to note that the impact of AI on employment is not solely negative. The section acknowledges that new job opportunities can also emerge due to AI technologies, particularly in AI-related fields that require specialised skills and expertise.

The section delves into the dynamics of job creation and destruction in the context of AI, considering factors such as technological advancements, market demands, and shifting skill requirements. It explores the concept of "job polarisation," where the middle-skill jobs susceptible to automation may experience a decline while high-skill and low-skill jobs see relatively more growth. The discussion also considers the potential for job displacement across different industries and the implications for workers in those sectors.

One of the key challenges highlighted in this section is the need for reskilling and upskilling the workforce to adapt to the changing demands of the AI-driven economy. As specific tasks become automated, there is a growing demand for workers with skills that complement and collaborate with AI systems. The section explores the importance of investing in training programs, educational initiatives, and lifelong learning opportunities to equip workers with the necessary skills for the AI era. It emphasises the need for proactive measures to ensure workers can access the resources and support needed to transition to new roles and industries.

Policy interventions and initiatives to support workers in the face of AI-driven changes are also discussed. This may include measures such as providing unemployment benefits, job placement services, and financial support for reskilling and upskilling programs. The section emphasises the importance of comprehensive policies that address the immediate needs of displaced workers and the long-term strategies for workforce adaptation in the AI era. It highlights the role of collaboration between governments, educational institutions, businesses, and other stakeholders in implementing effective support mechanisms.

8.2 Economic Inequalities and the Digital Divide

Integrating AI into the economy can exacerbate economic inequalities and create new divisions. This section explores the potential impact of AI on income distribution, access to opportunities, and socioeconomic disparities.

The discussion begins by examining how AI technologies can contribute to economic inequalities. It acknowledges that those with access to AI tools, resources, and skills may benefit disproportionately, leading to a concentration of wealth and power among particular individuals or groups. The section explores the potential consequences of these economic inequalities, including reduced job opportunities for specific population segments and limited access to AI's benefits.

To address these challenges, the section emphasises the importance of ensuring equitable access to AI technologies. It discusses the significance of promoting digital literacy and inclusion to bridge the digital divide. Efforts to provide equal opportunities for individuals to acquire AI skills and knowledge, regardless of socioeconomic background, are explored. The section highlights the importance of educational programs, community centres, and public-private partnerships in fostering digital inclusivity and reducing inequalities.

Moreover, the section examines the potential role of AI in addressing economic inequalities. It explores how AI technologies can be leveraged to create more inclusive and accessible services, improve resource allocation, and enable economic empowerment. The discussion emphasises the importance of considering ethical considerations in AI development to ensure that the benefits of AI are distributed equitably and contribute to reducing socioeconomic disparities. It highlights the need for policies and initiatives prioritising social impact and inclusivity in AI deployment.

8.3 AI and Economic Growth

This section focuses on the potential of AI to drive economic growth and innovation. It explores the various economic benefits that AI can bring, including productivity gains, new business models, and increased competitiveness.

The discussion begins by highlighting how AI technologies can enhance productivity in various sectors. By automating routine tasks, AI can free up human resources for more complex and value-added activities, increasing efficiency and output. The section explores case studies and real-world examples demonstrating how AI has already contributed to significant productivity improvements in manufacturing, logistics, and customer service.

The section also examines the role of AI in fostering innovation and the emergence of new business models. AI technologies can enable businesses to gain insights from large amounts of data, identify patterns and trends, and make data-driven decisions. This can lead to the development of innovative products and services, as well as the optimisation of existing processes. The discussion explores the potential for AI to drive entrepreneurship and the creation of AI-based startups that bring disruptive solutions to the market.

Additionally, the section discusses how AI can enhance competitiveness at both the organisational and national levels. AI technologies can provide organisations with a competitive edge by enabling them to offer personalised experiences, optimise supply chains, and make strategic decisions based on predictive analytics. At the national level, adopting and integrating AI can contribute to a country's economic competitiveness by attracting investments, fostering innovation ecosystems, and creating job opportunities.

The section emphasises the importance of creating an enabling environment for AI-driven economic growth. This includes investing in AI research and development, supporting AI startups and innovation hubs, and implementing policies promoting AI adoption and diffusion. It also emphasises the need to address challenges such as workforce adaptation, ethical considerations, and regulatory frameworks to ensure the sustainable and responsible deployment of AI technologies for economic growth.

Recommendations for the Future

9.1 For Policymakers

As AI continues to evolve rapidly, policymakers hold a crucial position in shaping a future where technological progress aligns with societal well-being and democratic values. The pace of AI innovation demands a shift away from static and reactive legal frameworks toward agile, dynamic, and anticipatory governance models. Policymakers should embrace regulatory approaches that evolve alongside technological change, incorporating frequent review cycles, feedback loops from diverse stakeholders, and regulatory sandboxes that allow for experimentation in a controlled environment. These tools can help balance innovation with risk mitigation, encouraging responsible development while ensuring public protection.

Central to AI governance is the need for enforceable transparency. Regulatory bodies should mandate that companies disclose detailed information about AI system architecture, training data provenance, decision-making logic, and post-deployment behaviour. High-impact use cases—such as facial recognition, predictive policing, autonomous weapons, and algorithmic credit scoring—require especially rigorous scrutiny.

Independent algorithmic audits, standardized impact assessments, and algorithm registries are essential tools for holding developers accountable and ensuring that AI systems meet safety, fairness, and human rights standards.

Public education must also become a foundational element of AI policy. Government investment in national AI literacy campaigns—spanning primary education to adult retraining—is necessary to equip citizens with the knowledge to understand and evaluate the AI systems they encounter daily. Policymakers should integrate digital and AI ethics education into public school curricula, provide funding for open-access educational platforms, and support partnerships with universities, libraries, and local non-profits to foster lifelong digital learning.

In addition, governments must implement data governance policies that prioritize individual privacy, data ownership rights, and equitable access to data resources. These policies should be technologically informed and guided by democratic principles, including data sovereignty for Indigenous and marginalized communities. Global coordination is key; international alignment on AI norms, best practices, and regulatory standards through frameworks like the OECD AI Principles, UNESCO's AI ethics recommendations, and the G7 Hiroshima Process will help ensure global consistency, avoid regulatory fragmentation, and promote ethical innovation worldwide.

Policymakers must also actively support public-sector AI adoption. Governments can model responsible AI deployment by implementing ethical procurement standards, conducting internal bias reviews, and ensuring transparency in the use of AI for public services like benefits administration, predictive analytics in policing, and pandemic response. Leading by example will foster public trust and demonstrate a commitment to equitable technological stewardship.

9.2 For Industry

The private sector remains the primary engine of AI innovation, making industry a powerful actor in shaping the trajectory of artificial intelligence. With this influence comes a responsibility to prioritize ethical design, long-term societal impact, and inclusivity at every phase of AI development. To build systems that serve the public good, industry leaders must embed human-centred values into the core of technological design—creating tools that enhance, rather than displace, human judgment, creativity, and agency.

To operationalize ethical principles, companies should establish cross-functional AI governance teams responsible for monitoring fairness, transparency, explain ability, privacy, and safety. These teams should work alongside product developers to conduct risk assessments, impact evaluations, and real-time monitoring for harmful outcomes. Frameworks like "Ethics by Design" and "Value-Sensitive Design" provide guidance for aligning AI development with diverse stakeholder values, and should be adapted into company workflows.

Financial investment in long-term AI ethics research and internal training for employees is also critical. Companies should allocate resources for bias mitigation, interpretability research, and algorithmic accountability initiatives. Incentivising ethical practices through executive compensation, ESG (Environmental, Social, and Governance) metrics, and internal recognition systems can embed these values deeper into corporate culture.

Inclusion should extend beyond diverse datasets. Teams building AI systems must themselves reflect a plurality of experiences and perspectives. This includes hiring practices that promote gender, racial, and cultural diversity, as well as involving civil society organizations, advocacy groups, and impacted communities in system design and review processes. Co-designing technologies with users—especially vulnerable or historically marginalized groups—can help prevent harm and ensure products are contextually relevant.

The private sector should also champion transparency through voluntary disclosure initiatives, open-sourcing AI tools when feasible, and collaborating with academic institutions to publish peer-reviewed research. Participating in industry consortia focused on responsible AI development, such as the Partnership on AI or the Global Partnership on AI, enables companies to help shape ethical standards and promote global interoperability. Ultimately, by taking leadership in responsible innovation, industry can earn the trust of users, regulators, and society at large.

9.3 For Educators and Individuals

Educators and individuals form the cultural and intellectual foundation for a society capable of navigating AI-driven transformation. In classrooms, universities, training centres, and informal learning spaces, the conversation around AI must extend beyond technical training to include critical thinking, civic responsibility, and ethical reflection. Educational systems at all levels must emphasize interdisciplinary learning that blends computer science with social science, philosophy, history, literature, and the arts. This holistic approach will empower students to understand AI not only as a tool, but as a force shaping culture, labour, governance, and identity.

Courses on algorithmic bias, data ethics, digital rights, and the history of technology should be integrated into general education requirements, ensuring all students—regardless of major—are equipped to engage with AI as informed citizens. Project-based learning that explores real-world challenges—such as misinformation, automation, or digital inclusion—can help learners connect abstract concepts to pressing societal issues. Public universities and community colleges have a unique opportunity to lead in this space, especially when they collaborate with local governments and businesses to co-design accessible AI literacy initiatives.

For individuals, embracing AI means developing a mindset of lifelong learning. This includes staying informed about AI developments through reliable news sources, engaging in public forums, and taking advantage of open educational resources. Individuals should explore how AI tools can augment personal creativity, decision-making, and productivity—while remaining critical of over-reliance, algorithmic bias, and data misuse. Understanding how to evaluate sources, detect deep fakes, and interpret algorithmic decisions is becoming as essential as reading and writing in the digital age.

Parents, caregivers, and community leaders can also play a role in fostering healthy AI engagement. This means encouraging media literacy in children, modelling balanced technology use, and initiating conversations about how AI affects relationships, identity, and social norms. Peer-to-peer learning communities—both online and in person—can support digital inclusion, especially for older adults and underserved populations who may feel alienated from emerging technologies.

Ultimately, a society of empowered educators and informed individuals is essential for ensuring that AI supports, rather than undermines, democratic values and human dignity. By cultivating curiosity, creativity, and ethical awareness, people at every level of society can help steer the future of AI toward equity, resilience, and collective flourishing.

Conclusion

AI's evolution between 2023 and 2025 marks one of the most rapid and consequential shifts in technological history—comparable to the Industrial Revolution in scale and to the advent of the Internet in global reach. In just two years, artificial intelligence has transitioned from a promising technological advancement to a foundational infrastructure underpinning critical sectors of modern society. AI now influences everything from education and healthcare to law, media, agriculture, defence, governance, and the global economy. Its capabilities have expanded far beyond automation, becoming tools for content generation, diagnostics, decision support, artistic collaboration, and personalized learning. This transformation has unlocked immense benefits: enhanced productivity, accelerated scientific discovery, improved accessibility of essential services, and the emergence of entirely new forms of human-machine synergy.

In creative sectors, AI is not only assisting musicians in composing new sounds or visual artists in generating novel aesthetics—it is redefining what creativity means in a world where algorithms can write poetry, simulate voices, and design entire virtual worlds. In science and medicine, AI is helping identify disease biomarkers, model climate change impacts, and design next-generation materials. It's playing a role in humanitarian work, assisting with disaster prediction, resource allocation, and refugee support. Yet, as AI becomes increasingly embedded in our infrastructure, homes, workplaces, and institutions, the boundaries between human and machine roles are becoming fluid—raising complex questions about authorship, identity, autonomy, and moral responsibility.

However, this unprecedented progress is shadowed by an equally vast array of emerging risks. Algorithmic bias continues to manifest in policing, finance, hiring, and healthcare systems—exacerbating existing inequalities. Job displacement, particularly in administrative, creative, and service sectors, is accelerating faster than many workforce adaptation efforts can keep pace with. Surveillance creep—through facial recognition, behavioural prediction, and real-time tracking—is infringing on civil liberties worldwide. Meanwhile, misinformation, enabled by AI-generated deep fakes and synthetic media, is undermining public trust in institutions, elections, and journalism. The centralization of AI power in a handful of global tech companies poses additional threats to innovation diversity, democratic accountability, and equitable access to benefits.

The rapid pace of AI deployment has often outstripped the capacity of institutions to anticipate or manage its effects. Regulatory frameworks lag behind technological innovation, and ethical guidelines are still catching up to the complexity and scale of current models. Without proactive intervention, AI could reshape societies in ways that are opaque, exclusionary, and destabilizing. The risk is not merely technical malfunction—it is the slow, cumulative erosion of trust, agency, and fairness in digital life.

Navigating the road ahead requires more than technological optimism—it demands collective vigilance, inclusive governance, and a sustained commitment to placing human dignity, justice, and sustainability at the centre of technological progress. Policymakers, industry leaders, civil society, and everyday citizens must work together to develop robust mechanisms for oversight, transparency, and accountability. This includes reimagining how AI is governed, how risk is assessed, and how power is distributed across stakeholders. Global cooperation will be essential—not only to harmonize regulation but to ensure the responsible development and equitable distribution of AI capabilities. Cross-border challenges such as algorithmic misinformation, autonomous weapon systems, and the export of surveillance technologies must be addressed with shared norms and enforceable agreements grounded in international law and human rights.

This moment, like previous technological revolutions, is an inflection point—a time to reevaluate what we value, how we define progress, and who gets to participate in shaping the future. History teaches us that unchecked innovation can widen inequality, entrench injustice, and amplify exploitation. But it also shows that coordinated, inclusive action can steer even the most disruptive technologies toward public good. By learning from the past—whether the environmental degradation of industrialization, the privacy invasions of the early Internet, or the monopolistic dynamics of digital platforms—we are better equipped to act decisively in the present.

To build a just and resilient AI future, we must invest in digital and algorithmic literacy, empower educators and learners, support lifelong reskilling, and expand civic dialogue around

AI's role in everyday life. Governments must prioritize equitable access to AI infrastructure and education. Developers must embed ethics, safety, and inclusivity into every layer of system design. And communities must be given meaningful voice and agency in how AI tools affect their lives.

We must also challenge dominant narratives that portray AI as inevitable, neutral, or infallible. AI is shaped by human intention—it reflects our goals, our data, and our societal structures. It is not a destiny, but a decision. Every dataset curated, every model trained, and every policy enacted represents a choice. By centring transparency, accountability, and empathy, we can ensure those choices are made with foresight and fairness.

Ultimately, the future of AI is not predetermined. It is being written now—in boardrooms and classrooms, in legislation and codebases, in homes and research labs around the world. Whether AI becomes a tool of empowerment or control, of connection or division, will depend on the vision, courage, and care we bring to this pivotal moment. It requires that we look beyond the immediate benefits of automation and efficiency and consider how AI reshapes the structures of power, culture, and human relationships. Thoughtful leadership must include a willingness to challenge market-driven priorities, close the digital divide, and anticipate unintended consequences before they take root. It means creating space for ethical deliberation at every level—from boardroom decisions to classroom debates.

Inclusive innovation will not arise by accident—it must be intentionally cultivated through policy, education, funding, and representation. This involves ensuring that AI tools are designed with input from historically marginalized voices, that benefits are broadly distributed, and that global disparities in access and opportunity are addressed rather than reinforced. We must foster a technological ecosystem where shared knowledge, open collaboration, and democratic oversight are prioritized over competition, secrecy, and proprietary control.

With a steadfast focus on human well-being as our compass, we can imagine and build an AI future that upholds dignity, celebrates creativity, and enables human flourishing. This is not simply a matter of regulation or design—it is a collective act of vision and will. By approaching AI with humility, wisdom, and a commitment to justice, we can shape a future in which AI truly amplifies human potential, protects fundamental rights, and contributes to a more just, informed, and humane world—where technology serves humanity, and not the other way around.

www.ingramcontent.com/pod-product-compliance
Lightning Source LLC
LaVergne TN
LVHW090431210926
848480LV00002B/784
* 9 7 9 8 2 3 0 0 2 3 4 1 8 *